Rosa Parks
Mother of the Civil Rights Movement

Roz Morris

Seacoast Publishing
Birmingham, Alabama

Rosa Parks: Mother of the Civil Rights Movement

Published by Seacoast Publishing, Inc.
1149 Mountain Oaks Drive
Birmingham, Alabama 35226

Copyright © 2003 Roz Morris

All rights reserved.
Reviewers and writers of magazine and newspaper articles are free to quote passages of this book as needed for their work. Otherwise, no part of this book may be reproduced or transmitted in any form or by any means, electronic or mechanical, including photocopying, recording or by any information storage and retrieval system, without the written permission of the publisher.

Library of Congress Control Number: 2002112976

Cover art by Thomas B. Moore

ISBN 1-878561-57-X

To obtain copies of this book, please write or call:
Seacoast Publishing, Inc.
Post Office Box 26492
Birmingham, Alabama 35260
(205) 979-2909

Dedication

In loving memory of my father, James E. (Rat) Collins

Special thanks to J. Mac Barber who wrote these words about my dad:

"Of his legacies, he was:

a good and decent person, who saw wrong and tried to right it;

who saw suffering and tried to heal it;

who saw brotherhood and tried to live it."

About The Series

Alabama Roots is a book series designed to provide reading pleasure for young people, to allow readers to better know the men and women who shaped the State of Alabama, and to fill a much-needed void of quality regional non-fiction for students in middle grades.

For years, teachers and librarians have searched for quality biographies about famous people from Alabama. This series is a response to that search. The series will cover a span of time from pre-statehood through the modern day.

The goal of *Alabama Roots* is to provide biographies that are historically accurate and as interesting as the characters whose lives they explore.

The *Alabama Roots* mark assures readers and educators of consistent quality in research, composition, and presentation.

It is a joint publishing project of Seacoast Publishing, Inc., and Will Publishing, Inc., both located in Birmingham, Alabama.

Some photos in the book are from The Highlander School.

Roz Morris

Researching Rosa Parks

As with all books, there was research to be done. Frankly, the only thing that I knew about Rosa Parks when I started this story was that she had refused to give up her seat on the bus in Montgomery. I began by gathering written research at Hoover Public Library, near where I live. Then, I read everything that I could find on the Internet.

I also read a lot of books about Rosa Parks. One of my best resources was the book *Rosa Parks: My Story*, written by Rosa Parks with Jim Haskins. I found many interesting stories about her childhood. In all, I looked at almost two dozen books about Rosa Parks, some were for young children and some were for adults. The ones that were most helpful were *Quiet Strength* by Rosa Parks with Gregory J. Reed, *Dear Mrs. Parks: A Dialogue With Today's Youth* by Rosa Parks with Gregory J. Reed, *Jumpin' Jim Crow* by Jane Elizabeth Dailey, *If A Bus Could Talk* by Faith Ringgold, *Voices of Freedom* by Henry Hampton, *Sisters In The Struggle: African American Women In The Civil Rights and Black Power Movement* edited by Bettye Collier-Thomas.

I spent a Sunday afternoon ay the Birmingham Public Library in the Southern History collection.

Rosa Parks: Mother of the Civil Rights Movement

There, I read articles from *The Birmingham News* and *Montgomery Advertiser* published in 1956 about the bus boycott, plus other articles about Rosa Parks.

Next, came the most fun part. I love field trips to find out about my characters. The new Rosa Parks Library and Museum had recently opened in Montgomery. I spent an afternoon touring the museum and gathering information. The most helpful things that I saw were the reenactment of Rosa refusing to give up her bus seat, and exhibits of the bus and of the kind of station wagon that was used to carry passengers during the boycott. The most interesting parts of all were the original historical documents such as her police fingerprint record, police mugshot and the court records from her arrest and trial.

After visiting the museum, I went to the Alabama Department of Archives and History. One of the workers there gave me names of people who had worked with Rosa Parks. I found personal reflections from them about their experiences with Mrs. Parks.

My biggest disappointment was that I didn't get to meet Mrs. Parks personally. Now that she is elderly, she seldom travels to Alabama and I was not able to travel to Detroit, Michigan to see her. However, I talked numerous times to helpful people at The Rosa and Raymond Parks Institute for Self-Development in Detroit to gather information and seek photographs.

Roz Morris

Contents

Prologue 8

Growing Up 11

The Klansmen Ride 17

Taking Care of Others 23

Going to School 27

First Trip to Montgomery 34

Montgomery Industrial School 40

Talking Back to White People 49

Raymond Parks Comes Calling 54

I Am Going To Vote! 63

The Highlander School 69

Rosa Goes To Jail 76

The Boycott Begins 90

Epilogue 101

Timeline 104

About the Author 109

Prologue

The scrawny black girl stood trembling with a brick in her hand.

"I dare you to hit me!" she shouted much more bravely than she felt.

The cocky white boy suddenly stopped his outburst of mean words. He had just threatened to hit her and this black girl amazed him. She was talking back to him and daring to pick up a brick. Black children shouldn't talk to white folks. Not like that. She should know that. What was wrong with her? Like a whipped dog, Franklin turned around and limped home.

Calmly, the young girl put the brick down and started home too. She didn't think anything more about the incident until the next morning.

"Grandmama, I saw Franklin yesterday," she said at breakfast. "He threatened to hit me, so I picked up a brick to hit him back."

Grandmama was usually calm. But at that moment

the fork dropped from her hand. "Rosa Louise McCauley, what do you mean?" she scolded. "You have got to learn that white folks are white folks. You just don't talk to white folks or act that way around them."

"But Grandmama, you've always said..." Rosa started to complain.

"No, Rosa. You don't do anything even if white folks do something to you. If you are peaceful, humble, and trusted, others will recognize that. If your life shows something else, that will be noticed in a bad way," Grandmama explained.

"That's just not right!" Rosa stormed. "You and Mama and Grandfather have always told me that people should stand up for their rights, just as the children of Israel stood up to Pharaoh."

Grandmama looked lovingly at the confused young girl. What she said was true. Yet, Grandmama knew that in 1923 in Pine Level, Alabama, such thoughts and actions could cause big problems.

"You are just too high strung!" Grand Mama explained. " If you aren't careful, you'll be lynched before you are twenty years old!"

Rosa knew that sometimes black people got hung for upsetting or being rude to white people. But, Grandmama's words stung. Rosa thought, *Grandma's*

Rosa Parks: Mother of the Civil Rights Movement

attitude is kind of a hurting thing because she is taking sides against what we really believe and me.

Rosa McCauley was only ten years old. Yet, she already felt a strong sense of what was fair. Later on, she'd realize that her grandmother scolded her because she was afraid for Rosa. "She knew it was dangerous for me to act as if I was just the same as Franklin or anybody else who was white."

On that morning, though, Grandmama's words were just a hurting thing. *Why would she take that white boy's side against me?* Rosa thought angrily.

Rosa didn't realize that her sense of fairness would lead her to greater battles with white people. She understood that she needed to find some way to stand up for her rights yet keep her behavior without blame. On this particular morning, she had no notion of how to do that. It never crossed her mind that she would be a big part of big changes in Alabama for black people.

Right then, she would never have believed it if someone told her she'd be known as "The Mother of the Civil Rights Movement." Right then, she was just an angry little girl who'd been done wrong.

And even her grandma wouldn't stand up for her.

Growing Up

ROSA LOUISE McCAULEY was born on February 4, 1913 in Tuskegee, Alabama. The scrawny, sickly baby quickly made Leona Edwards McCauley understand that she wasn't really prepared to be a mother. Leona was twenty-five years old and unhappy. Her husband, James McCauley, was a carpenter and builder and very good at making things with brick and stone. Leona and James had gotten married in Pine Level, Alabama, a tiny country town 20 miles southeast of Montgomery. The wedding was at Leona's home, on April 12, 1912.

Soon afterward, they moved to Tuskegee, a trip of 70 miles from Pine Level. "This will be a good place for us," James told Leona. "We can live close to Tuskegee Institute, the school for blacks. Tuskegee is known as a model of good race relations by both blacks and whites."

Leona agreed to the move because there were

Rosa Parks: Mother of the Civil Rights Movement

many building jobs for James. Also, she found a teaching job. Leona had attended Payne University in Selma long enough to get a teaching certificate, but not long enough to get a bachelor's degree. At that time, black teachers got paid less than white teachers, but the money was still better than what housekeepers got.

Soon after the move, Leona realized that she was going to have a baby. She was unhappy because James worked on building homes in different places in the county, and left her home alone a lot.

Actually, Tuskegee was a lot like Pine Level. Both towns were in Alabama's black belt, a narrow strip of prairie land wedged between the northern and southern parts of Alabama. The region got its name from the sticky black soil. It was a place of big cotton plantations. Even though the land around Tuskegee was like home, Leona was unhappy. "She had to quit teaching until after I was born, and she always talked about how unhappy she was, being an expectant mother and not knowing many people," Rosa later recalled.

Once Rosa was born, Leona spent a lot of time crying and wondering what she was going to do and how she was going to get along because she wasn't used to having a child to take care of. To make things worse, Robert, James' younger brother, came to live with Leona and James while he went to Tuskegee

Institute to take courses in carpentry and building. That meant one more person for Leona to cook and wash for, and she couldn't even teach anymore.

As unhappy as she was, Leona wanted to stay in Tuskegee. She knew it was the best place in all of Alabama for black people to get an education. So, she came up with a plan.

"James, what would you think about taking a teaching job at Tuskegee Institute?" Leona asked hopefully. "Just think, we'd be given a house to live in and Rosa would get an opportunity to get an education at the Institute when she's old enough."

James shook his head. "Leona, I don't want to teach at the Institute. I want to do contracting work, so that I can make more money. In fact, I think we ought to move back with my family in Abbeville."

Abbeville!

That was many miles south of Pine Level. Leona would be going even farther away from home.

Leona and James McCauley didn't agree on planning for the future. She had no choice. They went to Abbeville to live with James' family.

"It was a big family, with lots of children," Rosa recalled. One of her favorites was her uncle George Gaines McCauley, who was eight years older than Rosa.

Rosa Parks: Mother of the Civil Rights Movement

Rosa learned all she ever knew about her father's family from her young Uncle George. "He said that my father's grandfather was unknown and someone said he was one of the Yankee soldiers who served in the South during the Civil War. My father's grandmother was a slave girl and part Indian or something."

Leona never told Rosa much about her father's family. And, she and Rosa didn't stay in Abbeville long enough for Rosa to find out much about them.

"Leona, I need to go up north for a while," James said one day. "I can get some good building work up there. You and Rosa can stay with my family while I am gone."

"James, I don't want to stay here," Leona said. "Now that I'm going to have another baby, I want us to get settled and stay in one place."

Leona and James just couldn't seem to bring their lives together. He wanted to travel, and she wanted to settle down.

James left anyway. But Leona and Rosa did not stay with his family.

Soon after he left for work up north, Leona took little Rosa to live with her parents in Pine Level.

After a time, James came back to Alabama and joined the family in Pine Level and stayed until Rosa was two and a half years old.

He couldn't settle down, though. He wanted to travel to look for work, so he left. "I did not see him again until I was five years old and my brother was three," Rosa remembered. "He stayed several days and left again. This time he left for good.

"I did not see my father anymore until I was an adult and married," said Rosa.

So, most of Rosa's growing up memories are about her life with her mother, grandmother, and grandfather.

Her grandfather was the man in her home, and who was a father to her. "My earliest memory is of my grandfather taking me to the doctor to look at my throat," Rosa said. "I had chronic tonsillitis all through my childhood, but this was very early."

Rosa's grandfather took her to a store because there wasn't a doctor's office for black people in Pine Level. Grandfather sat Rosa on the counter in her little red velvet coat and bonnet. The doctor told Rosa to open her mouth, so she did.

"I can recall that everything the doctor asked me to do I just obeyed very nicely," said Rosa. "The people were amazed, with my being so small and being so little trouble. When Grandfather took me

Rosa Parks: Mother of the Civil Rights Movement

back home, he told my mother and grandmother about how well-behaved I was."

Rosa smiled, "That's the first time I can remember anything at all about myself. I always liked to be praised for any little thing. I felt kind of happy because he thought I was such a good little girl."

The Klansmen Ride

ROSA'S GREAT GRANDFATHER'S LAST NAME was Percival. The young Scotch-Irish boy came to the United States on a ship. He was white, but he wasn't free.

In those days, many poor white people who came to America from Europe signed agreements to work for someone for a few years in exchange for their fare to America. These poor white people had no rights and were treated as poorly as slaves. They were called indentured servants.

James Percival was indentured to some people in Pine Level named Wright. Black slaves were required to take the last names of their white owners, but white indentured servants were not. So, James never changed his name from Percival.

He married Mary Jane Nobles, a black slave. She also was a midwife—a person who helped deliver and

Rosa Parks: Mother of the Civil Rights Movement

care for babies. James and Mary Jane had two daughters and a son before President Abraham Lincoln declared freedom from slavery. Later, they had six other children. Rose, Rosa's grandmother, was five years old when the Civil War ended. Rose told Rosa many interesting stories about slavery.

She told Rosa how the slave owners had the slaves dig holes and bury many of the slave owner's most valuable household possessions—dishes, silver and jewelry—before the Yankees arrived. The slave children who were too young to dig, like Rosa's grandmother, were then sent to sit and play on the freshly dug soil to pack it down.

After the Civil War ended, so did slavery. Rosa's great-grandparents saved their money and bought twelve acres of land. Her great-grandfather built a little table so his family would have something to eat on.

Rosa's grandmother was six years old at the time, and the oldest child. She held a burning pine knot so her father could see to work at night building the table. "I still use that table today," Rosa said many years later.

Rosa also learned about her grandfather's family. His father was a white plantation owner named John Edwards, and his mother was a slave housekeeper and seamstress. She died when Rosa's grandfather, Sylvester, was young, and soon John Edwards died too. After that, Sylvester was treated very badly.

A man named Battle had been the overseer of the plantation for John Edwards. After Edwards died, Battle took over the plantation. He disliked Sylvester because he was the son of the plantation owner and a slave. In fact, he disliked Sylvester so much that every time he saw him he beat him.

The only food Sylvester remembered getting was the scraps the kitchen workers would slip to him. "The overseer tried to starve him, wouldn't let him have any shoes, and treated him so badly that he hated white people."

Sylvester taught his children, including Rosa's mother Leona, that they should never put up with bad treatment from anybody. Leona believed what her father taught and taught it to her own daughter, Rosa.

"My grandfather had a somewhat belligerent attitude toward whites in general," Rosa recalled. "And he liked to laugh at whites behind their backs."

Rosa remembers her grandfather being very emotional and excitable. "He didn't want my brother and me to play with white children. He made us stay away from them."

At the same time, Sylvester liked to take advan-

Rosa Parks: Mother of the Civil Rights Movement

tage of having very pale skin, of having others think he was a white person. He would introduce himself to a white man by saying, "Edwards is my name," and shake hands. At that time no white man would shake hands with a black man. Also, black men weren't supposed to introduce themselves by their last names.

The one thing that Sylvester wanted most was for none of his children to ever have to cook or clean for white people. That was why Leona had gone to Payne University to get a teaching certificate. However, another daughter, Fannie, did just what Sylvester hadn't wanted. She left home and went to work in Montgomery in white people's homes.

By the time Rosa McCauley was six years old, she realized that black people were not actually free. There were "Jim Crow laws" that separated black people from white people in many ways. These laws had gotten their name from a white man named Thomas Rice. He was a musical performer in New York who wore blackface makeup and did a song-and-dance making fun of black people. He'd dress up and sing:

Come listen all you gals and boys,
I'm going to sing a little song.
My name is Jim Crow.
Weel about and turn about and do jis so,

Roz Morris

Eb'ry time I weel about I jump Jim Crow.

The "Jim Crow laws" were a way of keeping black people separate from white people. They had separate water fountains, public restrooms, and neighborhoods. Black people were not allowed to eat in white restaurants or lunch counters, and when they rode the bus, they had to sit in the back.

Living in the country town of Pine Level, Rosa wasn't exposed to these laws often. But, she knew they were there. But she found out another way that some white people wanted to show blacks that they didn't have any rights.

It was the Ku Klux Klan. The Klan members rode horses through the black community burning churches, beating up people, killing people. "At one point the violence was so bad that my grandfather kept his gun—a double-barreled shotgun—close by at all times," Rosa said later.

Rosa and her younger brother, Sylvester, were taught just what to do if the Klansmen broke into their house.

"Go to bed with your clothes on so you can be ready to run if you have to," grandfather said. "I don't know how long I'll last if they came breaking in here, but I'm getting the first one who comes through the door."

Rosa Parks: Mother of the Civil Rights Movement

Rosa's family lived right on the highway, really just a gravel road. The Klansmen often rode on that highway.

"I'm not going outside looking for any trouble," grandfather said, "but I am going to defend my home."

When times got bad and the Klansmen rode hard up and down that road in front of her house, Rosa thought about what might happen. *Whatever happens*, she thought, *I want to see it. I want to see him shoot that gun. I don't want to be caught asleep.*

Many nights, Rosa's grandfather would sit by the fire in his rocking chair. Rosa sat on the floor right beside him. Grandfather would have his gun close by, just in case. Luckily, the Klansmen never attacked the McCauley's home.

After a while, the violence ended. Even though things had quieted down, Rosa knew that black people still were not really free.

Roz Morris

Taking Care of Others

ROSA'S GRANDPARENTS OWNED eighteen acres of land. They had fruit, pecan, and walnut trees, a garden, chickens, and a few cows.

"We didn't have to buy many things at the stores," Rosa said. "My grandfather was the one who usually went to the stores, but sometimes my brother and I would ride in the wagon with him."

Grandfather had eggs to sell, and he traded them for whatever else the family needed but didn't have. He also sold chickens and calves. The little bit of money that the family earned was from Leona's teaching and from working on other people's land.

When Rosa was about six years old, she went to work. She was given a flour sack like the other children and expected to collect one or two pounds of cotton from the fields. She became a field hand.

As she grew older, Rosa sometimes picked cotton

Rosa Parks: Mother of the Civil Rights Movement

and other times chopped it—or hoed the weeds from around the cotton plants. She was paid fifty cents per day for chopping cotton and one dollar for every hundred pounds of cotton that she picked.

Picking and chopping cotton was hard work. Rosa's family had a saying that they worked "from can to can't."

"We'd work from when you can see (sun-up) to when you can't (sundown)," Rosa explained. "I never will forget how the sun just burned into me. The hot sand burned our feet whether or not we had our old work shoes on."

Usually, the field hands didn't wear shoes. They explained it this way: "Didn't nobody have shoes on but the hoss (horse) and the boss."

Even though the family worked hard, Rosa liked being with her grandparents.

Sometimes, they would take her fishing at the creek.

"Rosa, Grandfather and I are getting on up in age," Grandmama would say. "So, how about you bait the hooks for us?"

"I guess that's why they liked to take me fishing," Rosa said. "I'd get the worm and he could wiggle all he wanted to. All I had to do was get one end of him started on the hook. Some people used to hit the worms and kill them, but I always believed that the fish could see that worm moving on the hook and that they'd bite a lively worm much sooner than a dead one."

Rosa's brother Sylvester was two years and seven months younger than her. Of course, he loved to follow Rosa around all of the time. Whatever Rosa said, Sylvester tried to repeat. He was always getting into mischief and Rosa had to take up for him.

After Sylvester was born, Rosa's mother Leona went back to teaching. The Pine Level black school already had a teacher, so she took a job in Spring Hill, about eight miles away. It was too far to walk back and forth every day, so during the week Leona stayed with a family in Spring Hill.

Each week, Rosa watched sadly as Leona got into the wagon with Grandfather. She was too young to understand why her mama was going away.

"Is Mama Leona going to learn how to teach school?" Rosa asked her grandmother.

"No, she's been teaching school since before you were born," Grandmama replied. "She's just going away to teach school."

Even though Rosa understood, she still wasn't happy. One day, while her mother was away, Sylvester got into trouble with Grandmama.

"Sylvester, I'm going to give you a whipping," Grandmama said as she took up a little switch.

Rosa quickly jumped in to defend Sylvester. "Grandmama, please don't whip brother. He's just a little baby and he doesn't have no mama and no papa either."

Grandmama put the switch down and looked at Rosa. *What must that child think about her family?* Grandmama wondered. She decided not to whip Sylvester that day.

"I can remember what a mischievous little boy he was and how I got more whippings for not telling on things he did than I did for things I did myself," Rosa later said about her younger brother. "I never did get out of that attitude of trying to be protective of him."

That attitude of taking care of others while being punished herself was one that would have a big impact on Rosa when she grew up.

Roz Morris

Going to School

LITTLE ROSA WAS SO EXCITED. The fall harvest of 1919 was over. She was six years old and she was finally going to school! Rosa already knew how to read. Mama Leona taught her at home when she was three or four. Rosa loved reading, and she loved to count. She thought, *It will be something great to be able to take a book and sit down and read!*

Rosa strolled to the one-teacher black school in Pine Level. The other children she was walking with told her that white children got to ride a bus to school.

"Well," Rosa said cheerfully, determined not to let anything or anyone ruin her happy mood, "our little frame school house is just a short way from where I live."

"You'd better hurry up and quit dawdling," one of the other children scolded.

"Why? We have plenty of time before school starts," Rosa replied.

Rosa Parks: Mother of the Civil Rights Movement

"The white children's school bus will be coming along directly," said the older child.

"So what?" Rosa wanted to know.

"So, when they see us walking to school they throw trash out the window at us," said her friend.

Sure enough, a few minutes later, the white children's bus lumbered down the road.

"Get out of the way!" yelled some of the white children as they chunked garbage out the window.

The older black children ran away from the road into the fields.

"Watch 'em scatter!" Rosa heard a white child taunt.

Once the bus passed by, Rosa was furious. Her best dress made by Grandmama was dusty from running in the field. "Who can we tell about this?" Rosa wanted to know. "How can we make them stop?"

"Ain't nothing we can do, Rosa. You just have to get off the road so we can make it to school everyday."

Rosa mulled over that thought the rest of the way to school. She felt shy and uncertain as she crossed in front of her church, Mount Zion A.M.E. Church, over to the school house that was right in the church yard.

The frame schoolhouse didn't have glass windows. There were wooden shutters instead. There was a wood-burning stove in the middle of the one big room. The larger boys had the chore of cutting wood for the stove and bringing it in.

"Come in and sit in the row with the other children your age," instructed Miss Sally Hill. Rosa looked curiously at her teacher.

Miss Hill was a light-brown-skinned lady with really large eyes. Those eyes seemed to show a lot of kindness.

Always wanting to do exactly as she was told, Rosa obediently sat on the row with the other six-year-olds.

"What is that baby doing here?" said a boy on the row behind Rosa.

Rosa knew she was small for her age. Mama Leona said it was because of her bad tonsils. She had even kept Rosa home from school a little longer than most of children. Rosa stared down at her tiny hands and tried to ignore the mean boy.

"Baby, do you think you can learn to read? Where's your mama, baby?" taunted the boy.

Rosa tried to blink back the tears. She felt her throat tighten, but no matter how she tried, the tears coursed down her cheeks.

"Come up here and sit by me, Rosa," said Miss

Rosa Parks: Mother of the Civil Rights Movement

Hill. "Are you glad to get to come to school?"

"Yes'm," Rosa replied shyly.

"We're going to learn many new things," said Miss Hill. "It will be fun."

"I already know how to read," Rosa replied a little more boldly.

"You do, do you?" smiled Miss Hill. "What do you like to read best?"

"I love fairy tales and Mother Goose rhymes," Rosa said. "I wonder, do you have Little Red Riding Hood? Somebody told me it was a nice book to read."

"We'll try to find it for you, Rosa," Miss Hill said as she patted Rosa's tiny hand.

After that time, whenever some of the other children would tease Rosa or say something about her size, she'd go up and sit by Miss Hill. Sometimes, Miss Hill called Rosa up to her desk just to talk to her.

The five months of the school year passed quickly.

"Next week will be our last one for the year," announced Miss Hill early one spring morning. "It's time for all of you to help your families plow and plant."

Rosa thought, *I wish we could go to school for nine months like the white children! I do love to learn.*

Rosa helped Grandmama and Grandfather plant

their fields. She worked long, hot days in the garden. When fall returned she helped harvest the crops and picked cotton again.

Finally, it was time to go back to school.

Sylvester was going to school with Rosa this year. As they started off to the schoolyard, Rosa looked lovingly at her little brother that she so fiercely protected. He was already larger than she and weighed more. Sylvester had eyes that were kind of slanted and he looked almost Oriental.

A man in town called Sylvester "Chink" because of his slanted eyes. It always made Sylvester angry.

The children hurried to get to school before the white children's school bus came along. Rosa was disappointed that Miss Hill wouldn't be back this year. Their teacher was going to be Mrs. Beulah McMillan. All of the children called her "Miss Beulah." She'd been a teacher for a long time and had taught Mama Leona when she was a girl.

Just the night before, Rosa had taken out the familiar picture of her mother in front of the same schoolhouse. She took Grandfather's magnifying glass to look closely at the faces that were very small.

Most of the children stood in rows on the steps in the front of the school. Some others stood on the ground. The shorter ones and the boys were on their knees on the ground. Mama Leona never wanted Rosa to show that picture to anybody because it was so battered up. But, Rosa liked it. *This year, I'll get my picture taken in front of the school with Miss Beulah just like Mama did!* Rosa thought.

Rosa liked school and she liked Miss Beulah. She thought, *School is a fun place to be!* She could hardly wait for recess time to come every day. The children dashed out to the school ground where the boys would play ball. Rosa was glad that the girls didn't play ball.

"If I try to be active, I fall down and get hurt," Rosa explained to Sylvester when he asked why she didn't like ball games. "I'm just not very good when it comes to running sports."

What Rosa did love at recess was what the girls called "ring games."

The girls sang rhymes and danced gaily around in a circle. One of Rosa's favorite ring games was "Little Sally Walker Sitting in a Saucer," where one girl sat in the middle as the others circled around and chanted the song. Other favorites were " Rise, Sally, Rise" and "Ring Around the Roses."

Rosa enjoyed her two school years at the Pine Level School. Pine Level was her whole world.

Little did she know that this, her second year

there, would be her last.

By the next school term Rosa would be in the big city of Montgomery!

First Trip to Montgomery

LEONA KEPT HER TEACHER'S LICENSE up to date by going to summer school at Alabama State Normal in Montgomery, a black teachers' college that is now Alabama State University. When Rosa finished her second year of school at Pine Level, Mama Leona decided that she was old enough to go along with her.

Rosa had never before been to the big city of Montgomery!

"Are you ready, baby? Do you have everything?" Mama Leona asked as she peered down the gravel road. "Mr. Barefoot will be here any minute."

Leona and Rosa were traveling to Montgomery in Mr. Barefoot's little Model T Ford. Black people paid him to take them places with his car service. Sometimes his car got crowded, but Rosa wasn't worried. She was just excited to be going to Montgomery.

"Now, Leona, you do remember how to get to

Cousin Ida Nobles' house, don't you?" Grandmama worried.

"Yes, Mother, I do," Leona replied.

"Mama Leona, I want to go, too!" whined Sylvester.

"Sylvester, we've already gone over this," Mama Leona patiently explained. "You're too little to go this summer. You've got to stay home with Grandmama and Grandfather."

Rosa felt sorry for her little brother, but not enough to dampen her excitement. She eagerly jumped into Mr. Barefoot's car with Mama Leona and waved good-bye.

To pass the time as they rode along, Mama Leona told Rosa about Cousin Ida. "She is really your Grandma Rose's first cousin," Mama Leona explained. "Her nephew, Gus Delaney, lives in the house with her, too."

"Where is his mama?" Rosa wanted to know.

"She went to Chicago several years ago and got killed by a streetcar, really sad thing," Mama sighed. "Anyway, Cousin Ida took Gus in just like she's taking us in."

"Isn't it going to be crowded?" Rosa asked.

"Well, maybe," Mama Leona agreed. "But, it's the best we can do. Black people can't stay in downtown

Rosa Parks: Mother of the Civil Rights Movement

hotels or white people's boarding houses. Anyway, we don't have enough money to pay for even a colored boarding house. So, Cousin Ida has agreed to take us in."

Rosa thought that sounded like a very kind thing to do. As soon as they got to the house, Leona introduced Rosa to Cousin Ida.

Rosa used her best manners for this kind lady who was about to take them in for the summer. "I am very pleased to meet you," she said.

Cousin Ida looked at Leona and said, "This is a special little girl. I like her very much."

Rosa loved that summer. Her mother took her to the laboratory school where the student teachers could get teaching practice while Leona went to classes. Rosa was always healthier in the summer and didn't have to miss as many days because of illness.

Alabama Normal seemed really big to Rosa compared to her little school at Pine Level. There was one big brick building called Tullibody Hall and four smaller buildings. There was an open field with bleachers for sports. Rosa thought, *This is going to be a wonderful adventure!*

After a few weeks in Montgomery, Rosa overheard Mama Leona and Cousin Ida talking.

"Leona, you know I've taken a liking to that little girl," Cousin Ida said. "I'd like her to stay here in Montgomery so she can go to school nine months out of the year. She can live right here with me."

Mama Leona agreed, "It'd be wonderful for her to have more schooling, and you do have a medical doctor right next door. If her throat or tonsils hurt, you could get help right away."

Rosa went to bed that night thinking about what it was going to be like to stay with Cousin Ida during the school year. She knew that Mama Leona thought it was an ideal situation.

So, it was a big surprise the next morning for Rosa to see her bags packed and Mama Leona ready to leave.

"Where are we going?" Rosa asked.

"We're going over to stay with Cousins Lelar and Saphonia Percival," Mama Leona calmly replied as she finished gathering their things. "Cousin Lelar is Grandma Rose's nephew."

"What about my staying here to go to school next term?" Rosa asked.

"Don't ask questions, now, Rosa," Mama Leona cautioned. "It's just time for us to go."

Cousin Ida didn't even tell them good-bye as they left. Rosa didn't think any more about it as she quickly adjusted to life at the Percival house. They had three young children—Pauline, Claud, and a new baby named Morris. It was the first time Rosa remembered staying in a house with a new baby. She enjoyed it.

Summer passed quickly and it was time to go back to Pine Level.

Rosa wondered if she'd ever go to school in Montgomery.

Not until many years later did Rosa learn the reason for their quick move from Cousin Ida's house.

After Rosa had gone to bed that night, Mama Leona and Cousin Ida continued to talk.

"You know, I really like that little girl," Cousin Ida reminded Leona.

"Yes, and I appreciate you taking her in," Mama Leona replied.

"Well, I just think it's best if I adopt her and have her as my own child," Cousin Ida explained. "That way she can go to a public junior high school."

"What are you talking about, Ida?" Leona asked. "I'm certainly not willing to give Rosa up."

"Leona, you've got your hands full and not enough money as it is," Ida persisted. "I can just take in that little girl, adopt her, and change her name to Nobles and..."

"Ida, this discussion is over," Leona said. "I was

willing for Rosa to stay with you for the school term. But, I am not willing to give her up."

"Then, I don't guess she needs to stay," Ida argued.

Leona could see how unhappy Ida was over the situation. That was the reason she decided to move on to another cousin's house for the rest of the summer.

Just getting to go to school was a hard thing for a black child in 1921! Rosa was about to find it getting even harder.

Montgomery Industrial School

BAD NEWS AWAITED ROSA AND LEONA when they got back to Pine Level.

Mount Zion had closed up the little frame school building, and there would no longer be any school for the black children in Pine Level. The only way Rosa and Sylvester could go to school was to travel the eight miles to Spring Hill every day.

Mama Leona knew that route well since she was the teacher there. But, Mama stayed with black families during the week at Spring Hill and only came home on weekends. Rosa and Sylvester couldn't do that. They'd have to walk back and forth to school every day.

"Rosa, what do you think it's going to be like to have Mama Leona for our teacher?" Sylvester wondered.

"She's a fine teacher, Sylvester. She'll teach us many wonderful things," Rosa assured him. "Just think of all she's already taught you and me. Mama Leona has taught us not to judge people by the amount of money they have or the kind of house they live in or the clothes they wear. How many times have you heard her tell us that people should be judged by the respect they have for themselves and others? That's one of the most important lessons we'll ever learn."

Sylvester soon learned that Rosa was right. One of the things that Mama Leona most believed in was exercising at school.

"Boys and girls, it's time to go outside for our stretching exercises," Mama Leona announced during a break in the day.

The children clambered outside to get their exercise since they didn't have a gym. When they were indoors, Mama Leona was creative about teaching other things besides reading, writing, and studying skills. Rosa remembers, "We girls did sewing, crocheting, knitting, needleworking. We made baskets out of corn shucks and pine needles."

So Mama Leona became Rosa and Sylvester's teacher, and it remained that way until Rosa turned 11.

That's when the idea of Rosa going to school in Montgomery came up again.

But before anything happened, Mama Leona and

Grandmama made another decision. Rosa kept having problems with her tonsils. She missed school a lot especially in cold weather. Being out in the country in the cold and drafty Spring Hill church school caused Rosa to keep colds and sore throats all the time.

Mama Leona took Rosa to their doctor to see what he could do. "Mrs. Parks, Rosa's heart is too weak for me to put her to sleep with strong drugs," he explained. "I can do this operation with her sitting in a chair with just a mild medicine to help with the pain."

"No, I can't stand that!" Mama Leona declared. "That would hurt Rosa too much. I'm going to take her to Montgomery to see if the doctors there can do something."

Mama Leona's sister, Fannie, and her family lived in Montgomery. Aunt Fannie had a son, Thomas, who was a few months younger than Rosa. Thomas' tonsils were fine. But, Mama Leona and Aunt Fannie found out that they could get both children's tonsils removed for the price of one. So, they decided Thomas would have his tonsils out, too.

Rosa and Thomas spent two nights in Hale's infirmary where a white doctor removed their tonsils. As soon as they were ready to go home, Thomas felt great. He was up and about and back into mischief. Rosa was not. She couldn't see for several days because her eyes swelled so badly. Her throat ached for weeks. Mama Leona took her back to Pine Level to heal, and Rosa stayed sick for a long time.

Finally, she began to feel better. "I feel so good since my tonsils don't hurt anymore," Rosa admitted.

"Well, finally, you don't eat like a bird anymore," Grandmama grinned. "I'm so glad to see that you're beginning to grow like you should."

"I can't wait to get to go back to school!" Rosa said.

Leona planned to pay tuition for Rosa to go to Montgomery Industrial School. Most people in Montgomery just called it Miss White's School because Miss Alice L. White was the principal and co-founder. Miss White and all of the other teachers at the school were white. All of the students were black girls. Miss White was from Melrose, Massachusetts and all of the teachers were from the North.

White people in Montgomery didn't like white women coming south to teach black girls. They didn't want anything to do with Miss White and the other ladies. The school was burned down twice, but Miss White kept rebuilding and teaching. She even went to church with the black people. Finally, the white people in town left her alone. The school had been operating for many years when Leona enrolled Rosa.

"Rosa, when school starts up, you'll go stay with Aunt Fannie and her children," Mama Leona explained.

Rosa looked forward to living with her cousins Howard, Thomas, Annie Mae, and Ella Frances Williamson. Aunt Fannie's husband had died several years before.

Rosa eagerly awaited the move and her first day of school. "There's one thing that you should know before you go," Mama Leona warned. "I've talked to Miss White. Since you missed so much school with your tonsils and since you're coming from a country school, they think you might be behind the other children."

Miss White's school, where Rosa was a student

"But, Mama Leona, I'm not behind," Rosa protested.

"No matter," Mama Leona waved her slender hand. "They've decided to put you back into fifth grade instead of the sixth."

I'll just have to show them how smart I am! Rosa thought.

She was moved to the sixth grade in the middle of the first term of school.

Mr. Julius Rosenwald, president of Sears, Roebuck & Co., gave money to Miss White's school. He was interested in the education of black children in the South even though he was white. Because of the students' tuition and the money that Mr. Rosenwald and other organizations gave to the school, The Montgomery Industrial School wasn't a one-room schoolhouse. In fact, it was a three-story brick building. It still stands in Montgomery on Union Street close to High Street. This brick building is now a part of Booker T. Washington High School.

Rosa's cousins didn't get to go with her to Miss White's school. They went to a public junior high school for black children. But, Rosa and her cousins could walk to and from school together. If the weather was bad, they rode streetcars. The black people had to go as far back in the streetcar as they could. If too many white people wanted to ride and there weren't enough seats, the black people had to get off.

Rosa thought about the lesson Mama Leona had taught her. People should be judged by the respect they have for themselves and others, not for the money they have or the kind of house they live in or the kind of clothes they wear. They surely shouldn't be judged just because of the color of their skin. This rule is not right!

Rosa saw other things in Montgomery that made her angry. Public water fountains were one. These fountains had signs that said "White" and "Colored." Rosa knew she wasn't supposed to drink from a white fountain.

"Annie Mae, do you think white water is whiter and ours comes in different colors?" Rosa wondered. "Does theirs taste different?"

After a while Rosa realized that all water had the same color and taste. The only difference was who got to drink from which fountain. That just didn't seem right either.

One day, Rosa and Annie Mae and some other children were walking home from school. There was no way for them to get home without going through a white neighborhood. A white boy glided by on roller skates. Suddenly, as he passed Rosa, he tried to push her off the sidewalk.

Not remembering Grandma's harsh warning years before about the right way to treat white people, Rosa turned around and pushed him back.

A white lady was standing nearby. She turned out to be the boy's mother.

"Girl!" she yelled. "Don't you know that I can put you so far in jail that you won't ever get out? You better not ever push my child."

Boldly, Rosa explained, "But, ma'am, he pushed me and I don't like to be pushed either. I wasn't planning on bothering him at all."

Then, Rosa, Annie Mae, and the other children dashed to Aunt Fannie's house before the lady could say any more. Just as soon as Mama Leona heard about the incident, she decided that Rosa needed to move back with Cousin Lelar and Saphonia.

"Rosa, I don't want you passing through white neighborhoods to get to and from school every day. It is just too dangerous," she said.

So, Rosa packed up and moved back to her other cousin's house. At least, she still could go to Miss White's school. There were more than 250 girls at the school. They studied the usual school subjects like English and science and geography. Another class that

Rosa Parks: Mother of the Civil Rights Movement

Rosa enjoyed was domestic science. Here Rosa learned to cook and sew and take care of sick people. She had a textbook on how to look after patients in the home, make the beds, feed them, and give them whatever care they needed. Little did Rosa realize how much she'd need to know that information one day.

Right then, she just enjoyed learning that she was a person with dignity and self-respect who should not set her sights lower than anyone else's because she was black. She'd been learning that lesson all along at home, but is surely was nice to have white teachers to tell her the same thing.

Just when Rosa thought things couldn't get any better, Miss White got ill.

She couldn't find young teachers to come in and teach, and none of the other teachers felt like they could step in and take her place.

So, Miss White's school closed.

Rosa had just finished eighth grade.

Now what will I do? Rosa wondered nervously.

Roz Morris

Talking Back to White People

FOR ONCE, ROSA DIDN'T HAVE LONG to worry about where she would go to school.

The Swayne School, which had formerly been a white school, changed to Booker T. Washington Junior High for blacks. So, Rosa stayed in Montgomery for ninth grade.

By the time school started, Aunt Fannie had moved to a completely black neighborhood. The children wouldn't have to go through white neighborhoods to get to school. Leona wasn't so worried anymore. So Rosa moved back in with her family. Aunt Fannie cleaned at a Jewish country club in Montgomery and often took the children to help her work. The country club was in a white community. Nearby was a vacant lot full of blackberry briars.

"Rosa, let's go out in the lot and pick berries," Annie Mae said one day after they'd finished their

Rosa Parks: Mother of the Civil Rights Movement

chores for Aunt Fannie.

White people's houses backed up to the lot. When Rosa and Annie Mae started to pick the berries, a little boy watched them from his yard.

"You colored girls better leave them berries alone!" he ordered.

Rosa and Annie Mae weren't afraid of the little white boy. "You can't do nothing to us!" Rosa retorted.

"If you come over here, we'll give you a good beating," Annie Mae added.

The little boy ran into his house.

On the way home that evening, Rosa and Annie Mae told Aunt Fannie about the little boy and what they'd told him. They thought she'd laugh.

Instead, Aunt Fannie bellowed, "You all crazy? You keep your mouths shut. If he'd gone and told somebody, they would have had y'all lynched and all we could do was cry a little bit about it."

Rosa took in her second lesson on not talking back to white people. *At least this time it doesn't bother me as much because Annie Mae and I were in it together*, Rosa thought. *It's a whole lot harder to stand up to people all by yourself.*

Still, Rosa continued to stand up for herself and other black children when she thought she had to.

After a while, Sylvester came up from Pine Level and lived with Aunt Fannie, too. There were some woods behind Aunt Fannie's house with a creek running through it.

"You children run down to the creek and get some sticks for firewood," Aunt Fannie said one afternoon.

As the children gathered the sticks a crowd of teenage white boys started to taunt them.

"We're gonna throw this big darkie into the creek," jeered one of the boys as he pointed at Sylvester.

Sylvester wasn't nearly as large as any of the white boys. As always, Rosa felt she had to stand up for her baby brother.

Rosa dropped the sticks she was holding, put her hands on her hips, and shouted back, "Well you won't be putting nobody in the water unless all of us go in together!"

Surprisingly, the big boys backed down and walked away.

"You sure told them, Rosa," Sylvester beamed. "They didn't want no part of us pulling them in the water after us."

"Whatever y'all do, don't tell Aunt Fannie about this!" Rosa warned the other children. Talking back to

Rosa Parks: Mother of the Civil Rights Movement

white people was one thing. Letting her mother or Aunt Fannie know about it was quite another.

Rosa finished junior high and moved on to the laboratory school at Alabama Normal School for grades ten and eleven. By this time, it was called Alabama State Teachers' College for Negroes. There was still no public high school for blacks in Montgomery. Rosa loved school and everything about it. She planned to be a teacher just like Mama Leona.

During the fall of her eleventh grade, Rosa faced more bad news. Grandmama was sick. Rosa had to go home to take care of her. So Rosa dropped out of high school and went back to Pine Level. All of her training in patient care was put to use. She carefully tended to her Grandmama.

About a month after Rosa got home, Grandmama died. Rosa was sixteen years old, and she left Pine Level to go back to Montgomery and to her first real job. She went to work in a shirt factory making men's blue-denim work shirts. She tried to go back to Alabama State too.

After a short time, Mama Leona got sick. She had bad headaches and swelling in her feet and legs. There was only one thing for Rosa to do. Once again, she dropped out of school and quit her job making shirts to take care of Mama Leona. Sylvester went to work.

Years later, Rosa recalled, "I was not happy about dropping out of school either time, by it was my responsibility to help with my grandmother and later to take care of my mother. I didn't complain. It was just something that had to be done."

Even after Mama Leona got better, Rosa didn't go back to school. Someone had to run the farm in Pine Level, and tend to the house and do the chores.

Rosa felt like it was her job to tend to things.

The weight of all those grown-up things hung like heavy chains around Rosa's shoulders. *I don't guess I'll ever go back to school again*, she thought sadly.

But, there were many big changes ahead for Rosa McCauley.

Going back to school again might just be one of them.

Raymond Parks Comes Calling

IT WAS THE SPRING OF 1931. Rosa was in her late teens.

One of Rosa's lady friends insisted that there was a man she would like for Rosa to meet.

"I'm not a bit interested right now," Rosa insisted. "I've had some pretty unhappy romantic experiences already, and I've got too much to do."

Her friend didn't take no for an answer and introduced Rosa to Raymond Parks. It was an introduction that would bring big changes to Rosa's life.

Later, Rosa recalled, "I thought he was too white. I had an aversion to white men, with the exception of my grandfather, and Raymond Parks was very light skinned."

Raymond was twenty-eight and worked as a barber in a black barbershop in downtown Montgomery owned by Mr. O.L. Campbell. Rosa could tell that he was interested in her.

"I just spoke politely to him and didn't give him another thought," Rosa said.

Raymond had given Rosa another thought, though. He decided to try to look her up. He came driving down her road one afternoon. First, he asked an elderly lady if she knew Rosa McCauley.

What is a person like that doing looking for Rosa? the lady wondered. *It's not good for a white man to come around here asking questions.*

"No, sir," she respectfully replied. "I don't believe I know her."

Still, Parks—as everyone called him—didn't give up. Farther on down the road, he saw a lady standing on her porch with her hair in braids.

"Ma'am, do you know where Rosa McCauley lives?" he asked.

Leona McCauley replied, "As a matter of fact, I do. She's my daughter, and she lives right here."

Mama Leona invited Parks to come in. He sat and visited with the family for a little while. But, Rosa was still very shy and not at all interested in him. She thought, *Surely he'll go away this time because I'm so timid and don't have anything to say.*

Raymond Parks wouldn't give up. He came back to the house again. This time, Rosa wouldn't go out to see him. She went to bed and covered up and refused to come out.

"Well, if she's gone to bed, I won't stay," Parks told Mama Leona.

But, he came back again. Finally, Rosa agreed to go riding with him in his car, a little red Nash with a rumble seat that folded up and down in the back. It was very unusual for a black man to own his own car.

As Rosa and Parks drove along, she found that she enjoyed talking to him. He started to tell her about his life experiences. Rosa found out that Parks had been born in a place called Wedowee, Alabama, near Roanoke. He'd grown up in an all-white neighborhood, but he wasn't allowed to go to the school there because it was a white school. The black school was too far from his home, so his mother taught him to read and write at home. For a short time, he went to school in Roanoke, but he really hadn't had much formal schooling. He thought Rosa was very smart to have gone to school as much as she had.

Parks told Rosa about taking care of his sick mother and grandmother until they died. Then, he went to work taking care of the church and church grounds at a white Baptist church in Roanoke.

"Well, how did you end up coming to Montgomery?" Rosa asked one day as they were riding.

"They had just put shrubbery around the church and I was supposed to water it," Parks started to explain. "You know that you're not supposed to water plants in the heat of the day?"

"Oh, yes," Rosa quickly agreed.

Rosa as a young woman

"Well, I waited until the evening after the sun went down to do my watering," Parks explained. "Then, the wife of one of the church deacons told the pastor that I hadn't been watering the shrubs."

"What happened then?" Rosa asked.

"The pastor spoke to me about it and said that Mrs. Jones said I didn't water the shrubbery," Parks said. " I said that I did."

The pastor said, "Mrs. Jones told me you didn't water it, and if her husband knows you dispute her word, he will sweep up this churchyard with you."

Parks said, "I didn't water it in the middle of the

day but when I was supposed to, to keep the sun from scorching it. And Mr. and Mrs. Jones will not wipe up the churchyard with me and neither will you."

Rosa felt a chill go up her spine at the thought of a black man talking back to a white man like that.

"Even though I had a little sister at home, I knew it was time for me to leave," Parks said. " I asked one of my cousins to take care of her. I couldn't stay there. I had several jobs and moved around quite a bit. Finally, I spent some time in Tuskegee where I learned barbering. Then, I came here to work for Mr. Campbell."

Even though Parks made Rosa nervous because he was not afraid of white people, she was also impressed by his strong attitude.

"Parks was also the first real activist I ever met," Rosa said later. "He was a long-time member of the NAACP, the National Association for the Advancement of Colored People, when I met him."

Parks worked with other black men to raise money to help pay for the legal fees for "the Scottsboro Boys." They were nine young men who had been arrested and charged with attacking two white women. The boys ranged from fourteen to nineteen years old. They were found guilty of the crime on April 9, 1931 and all but the youngest were sentenced to die in the electric chair.

"I thought it was awful that they were condemned to die for a crime they did not commit," Rosa remembered. "By this time, the case had made the newspapers, and people outside the South were up in arms about the way the young men had been railroaded."

The trials and appeals for "the Scottsboro Boys" went on for years. Not until 1950 was the last accused man released.

Rosa knew that Parks was working for the Scottsboro Boys from the beginning. She admired his courage. "Later I came to understand that he was always interested in and willing to work for things that would improve life for his race, his family, and himself," Rosa said.

Not only did Rosa and Raymond talk about his life and his work. They also talked about getting married. One Sunday in August, when Rosa was at church, Parks asked her mother's permission to marry her. When Rosa got home from church, Leona said, "Parks has asked my permission for the two of you to get married and I agreed."

Rosa and Parks were married in December of 1932 in Pine Level. It was a small wedding with only family and close friends. After they got married, Rosa and Parks moved to Montgomery, not far from Ala-

Rosa Parks: Mother of the Civil Rights Movement

bama State, in a rooming house on South Jackson Street.

Rosa talked to Parks about her desire to finish school. She knew that he was interested in anything that would improve her life. So, Rosa went back to school once more and received her high school diploma in 1933 when she was twenty years old.

Even with a high school diploma, Rosa had trouble finding work. First, she worked as a helper at St. Margaret's Hospital and took in sewing on the side. Then, in 1941, she got a job at Maxwell Field, a nearby Air Force Base.

Throughout this time, Parks kept going to night meetings about the Scottsboro case. Rosa didn't go to the meetings because it was so dangerous. Whenever the meetings were held, someone was posted as a lookout, and someone else had a gun. Parks thought all of this was too dangerous for Rosa to get involved.

However, there was one meeting that Rosa remembers well. She and Parks had moved to a house on Huffman Street called a shotgun house. It was called this because if you shot a bullet, it would go through the whole house because of the way the rooms were lined up on either side of a long hall. The meeting that Rosa remembers was to be held at her little house.

"There was a little table about the size of a card table that they (the men) were sitting around. This was the first time I'd seen so few men with so many guns. The table was covered with guns. I didn't even think to offer them anything—refreshments or something to drink. But, with the table so covered with guns, I don't know where I would have put any refreshments. No one was thinking of food anyway.

"I can remember sitting on the back porch with my feet on the top step and putting my head down on my knees, and I didn't move throughout the whole meeting. I just sat there. After the meeting was over, I remember, my husband took me by the shoulders and kind of lifted me from the porch floor. I was very, very depressed about the fact that black men could not hold a meeting without fear of bodily injury or death. Also, I was reminded of the time I was a child and I sat next to my grandfather waiting for the Ku Klux Klan to ride down on us."

Another night, Parks had gone to a meeting and Rosa was sitting in the swing on their porch at their new house on South Union Street. Two motorcycle policemen kept going up and down the block. Rosa knew that the police were trying to find out where the people who were doing the late-night meeting lived and who they were. She was trembling so badly that

Rosa Parks: Mother of the Civil Rights Movement

the porch swing jingled. Rosa was worried about Parks.

Parks knew the police were patrolling his neighborhood. So, he came home on a little pathway from Bainbridge Street and in the back door.

"Next thing I knew, he was in the house," Rosa said. "So I felt better. At least they didn't get him that time."

Rosa admired Parks for his activism or willingness to stand up for a cause. Even though she approved of his courage, she couldn't help being afraid of what might happen to him. Never would Rosa imagine that one day, Parks would be admiring her activism and worrying about what could happen to her.

I Am Going To Vote!

ONE BENEFIT OF BEING AN AMERICAN is having the chance to vote.

To vote for or against taxes.

To allow governments to borrow money.

To decide on projects that governments undertake—whether to spend money for roads, bridges or schools and civic centers.

To choose the people to be governors, senators, representatives, mayors, council members, school board members, judges and county commissioners.

The problem was that a lot of white people in Alabama in the 1940s wanted to keep the voting privilege just for themselves.

They did not want to share it with black people.

So they set up rules that made it difficult for blacks to register to vote. Before they could register to vote, black people had to have white people to vouch

Rosa Parks: Mother of the Civil Rights Movement

for them.

Mr. Edgar Daniel Nixon was a black man in Montgomery who was working very hard to change the rules so it would be easier for black people to register to vote. Not only was he the president of the Brotherhood of Sleeping Car Porters, but he also was the president of the Montgomery Branch of the National Association for the Advancement of Colored People (NAACP). Mr. Nixon was a proud and dignified man. He stood tall and straight, with great pride. He fought to break down the barriers to voting for black people. Along with a New York lawyer, Mr. Arthur A. Madison, Mr. Nixon helped to teach black people about a test they would have to take to prove that they could read and write, so they could be approved to vote.

Rosa decided to register to vote. It was 1943. The registration books for voting were only open at a certain time, and if she couldn't find out when that was she would miss her chance. The first day that was selected for registration was a working day for Rosa, so she couldn't go. The next day, which was Rosa's day off from work, she went to register and take her test. She never received a certificate in the mail as evidence that she was a legally registered voter.

Rosa went back. "You didn't pass," she was told. Rosa felt sure she had done well on the test, but there was nothing she could do about it.

She tried again in 1944.

Rosa didn't pass then either, but she had an adventure that she would not forget.

She was thrown off a Montgomery city bus that she was trying to ride to the place where she had to take the voting test.

Sometimes in those days bus drivers made black passengers step in the front door of the bus to pay their fares, and then get off and go around to the back door to get on the bus. If the black passengers didn't get to the back door quickly enough, the bus would take off without them.

Each bus had thirty-six seats. The first ten were reserved for white people even if there were no white passengers on the bus. Black people were required to sit in the back of the bus even if there were empty seats up front. Once the back seats were filled, the rest of the black passengers had to stand. It was up to the bus driver to regulate the seating in the middle sixteen seats.

Some bus drivers were mean. They carried guns and had "police power" to rearrange the seating however they wanted. On the day that Rosa caught the bus to take the voting test, the driver was a man that many

Rosa Parks: Mother of the Civil Rights Movement

black people were afraid of. He was tall and thickset, a beefy man. His skin was rough and he had a mole near his mouth. His name was J.P. Blake.

As Rosa stepped into the front of the bus to pay her fare, she saw that the back was crowded with black people. They were even standing on the steps that led up from the back door. There were hardly any people at all in the front of the bus. So, Rosa got on at the front and walked straight to the back rather than getting off again.

"Get off the bus and go to the back door and get on," Mr. Blake hollered.

"I'm already on the bus," Rosa answered. "I don't see the need of getting off and getting back on when there are people standing in the stepwell. How could I squeeze on anyway back there?"

"If you can't go through the back door, you'll have to get off my bus," Mr. Blake insisted.

Rosa stood where she was. This was the most disobedient she'd ever been to a white person. Mr. Blake came back and took her coat sleeve. He led her to the front of the bus. Rosa dropped her purse. Rather than stoop over to get it, she sat right down in the front seat to pick it up. This made Mr. Blake even angrier.

Standing over Rosa, he shouted, "Get off my bus!"

"I will get off," Rosa said. She thought he looked as if he might hit her, so she added, "I know one thing. You better not hit me."

As Rosa got off the bus, she heard a black person mumble from the back, "How come she don't go around and get in the back?"

Others started to grumble as she was leaving the bus. "She ought to go around the back and get on." They wondered why she didn't act like the rest of the black people that day.

Since Rosa already had her transfer slip for the bus, she didn't try to get back on the same bus. She decided she'd wait for the next bus and a different driver. Rosa thought, *I never want to be on that man's bus again. I'll make a point of looking at who is driving the bus from now on before I ever get on. I don't want any more run-ins with this mean one.*

As much as Rosa wanted to avoid J.F. Blake, it would not be her last run-in with him.

To make matters worse, when Rosa finally got to the test site she failed again.

In 1945, Rosa took the test again. This time, she made a copy of the twenty-one questions and the answers she'd given. She carefully copied each question and answer by hand. She was so upset by the way

Rosa Parks: Mother of the Civil Rights Movement

she had been treated the first time she tried to register, she was ready to fight in court for her right to vote.

If her answers were right but she wasn't given the right to vote, she decided, she would file a lawsuit against the voter-registration board. But she did pass. Her certification arrived in the mail. She was a registered voter!

Next, Rosa found out that there was a poll tax of $1.50 a year that every registered voter had to pay. Black people had to pay it back to the time they were twenty-one, the legal age to vote in those days. In 1945, Rosa was thirty-two years old, so she had to pay $16.50, which was a lot of money for her. Rosa did it anyway because she was so anxious to be a registered voter.

She was going to vote!

Roz Morris

The Highlander School

BY THE TIME THAT ROSA was put off the bus in 1944, she had been a member of the NAACP for several months. Parks had been a member of the Montgomery branch for a long time, but he didn't want Rosa to join because he thought it was too dangerous.

Rosa didn't know there were any women in the NAACP until she saw a picture in the *Alabama Tribune*. There was Johnnie Carr, Rosa's friend and classmate from Miss White's school. The article said that Johnnie was working with the NAACP's Montgomery branch.

Maybe one time I'll go over to the NAACP and see if I can run into Johnnie, Rosa thought.

It was December, 1943, and the Montgomery chapter was having the annual election of officers meeting. Rosa decided to go. That day, Johnnie wasn't at the meeting, and there were only about a dozen men present. Rosa paid her membership dues and sat quietly to watch the elections.

One of the men turned to Rosa and said, "We need a secretary."

Since she was the only woman there and since she was too timid to say *no*, Rosa just started to take minutes of the meeting. That was the way she was elected secretary of the Montgomery Branch of the NAACP. Even though he was a little surprised, her husband Parks was encouraging about Rosa's new assignment.

Mr. E.D. Nixon was president of the chapter. He always complimented Rosa's work and encouraged her to continue. As secretary, Rosa recorded and sent membership payments to the national office. She answered telephones, wrote letters, and sent out press releases to the newspapers. One of her main duties was to keep a record of cases of unfair treatment against black people.

By 1949, Rosa was not only the secretary of the Senior Branch of the NAACP, she was also the adviser to the NAACP Youth Council. Rosa enjoyed working with young people. One of her projects was getting the young people to try to check out books from the main Montgomery library instead of going to the little branch across town that was known as the "colored library."

The colored library didn't have many books. If a student requested a book from the main library, he had to wait for it to be delivered to the colored library before he could pick it up. With Rosa's encouragement, the boys and girls of the NAACP Youth Council went to the main library to ask for service there. They were turned down again and again. Just like Rosa, they kept trying.

Mr. Nixon introduced Rosa to Mrs. Virginia Durr. Mrs. Durr was a white woman, born and raised in Birmingham. She and her husband, Clifford, a lawyer, did a lot for black people. Rosa met Mrs. Durr in 1954 at Mr. Nixon's home. When Virginia found out that Rosa could sew, she asked Rosa to help with her daughter Lucy's wedding wardrobe, called a trousseau.

By 1955, Rosa got to know Virginia Durr very well.

"I became aware of racism when I went off to college in Massachusetts," Virginia told Rosa. "One day I went to the dining room, and there was a black girl at the table I was assigned to. I had to make up my mind about sitting down next to a black person to eat. Over time, I realized that this young woman had the same right to sit there as the other students."

Rosa really liked what Virginia had to say. Virginia talked to her about the Supreme Court decision known as Brown versus Board of Education that was made in 1954. It was a decision to settle an argument in Little Rock, Arkansas, about whether black students should be allowed to go to school with white students. The ruling declared that segregation, or separating black people from white people, was against the United States Constitution. That meant it was legally wrong. At first, nothing much changed, though.

Virginia continued to talk to Rosa. She told her about a workshop that was going to be held at the Highlander Folk School in Monteagle, Tennessee. The workshop was called, "Racial Desegregation: Implementing the Supreme Court Decision."

"Rosa, there is a scholarship available to attend," Virginia told her. "I'll get together your expenses to go up there for this ten day workshop."

Mr. Nixon was anxious for Rosa to attend, too. Rosa went home full of ideas and plans.

"Parks, we have a wonderful opportunity," Rosa explained. "Why don't you go with me to this workshop?"

"I don't object to you going, Rosa," he replied, "but you know I don't like to travel away from home

Rosa, second from right, at Highlander Folk School workshop

that much."

By this time, Leona had come from Pine Level to live with Rosa and Parks. So Parks said, "Your mother and I can get along without you. I can cook."

So, in the summer of 1955, Rosa boarded a bus to Chattanooga, Tennessee. A white man picked her up at the bus station and drove her fifty miles to Monteagle. Even though Rosa and the white man didn't talk much, Rosa felt quite comfortable. The scenery was beautiful. The Highlander school was on a plateau in the mountains and surrounded by gardens and herds of cows.

Rosa Parks: Mother of the Civil Rights Movement

Rosa spent ten days at Highlander and went to many different workshops. She was forty-two years old and it was one of the first times in her life that she didn't feel hostility or unfriendliness from the white people.

"I experienced people of different races and backgrounds meeting together in workshops and living in peace and harmony," she said. "I felt that I could express myself honestly without any repercussions or antagonistic attitudes from other people."

At the end of the workshop, Rosa found it hard to leave. She knew she would be returning home to the Cleveland Avenue housing project where she and Parks lived. That part would be fine. The part that was

Cleveland Avenue housing project, where Rosa lived, as it appears today

not fine is that she would be returning to her job as an assistant tailor at Montgomery Fair department store. Rosa thought, *There I have to be smiling and polite no matter how rudely I'm treated. And I'll be back to those city buses with those segregation rules.*

Rosa came back to Montgomery from the workshops.

Her life was never the same again.

Rosa Goes To Jail

IN 1955, BLACK PEOPLE MADE UP more than sixty-six percent of Montgomery's bus riders.

That was a lot of business for the bus company.

Mr. E.D. Nixon knew that and he kept going to the bus company trying to get better service for the company's black riders. First, he went to complain about black people having to pay at the front door and then go around to the back door to enter. The managers at the bus company said, "Your folks started it. They do it because they want to."

Then Mr. Nixon asked if the route of the Day Street bus could be extended. Black people from a small community on the other side of the Day Street Bridge had to walk about half a mile to get to the bus. This time the bus people said, "As long as the people are willing to walk the half mile and to pay to ride the rest of the way downtown, there is no need to extend the bus line."

Jo Ann Robinson, an English professor at Alabama State College, helped found the Women's Political Council. Often, she led protests to the bus company. Finally, she managed to get the company to agree that the buses would stop at every corner in black neighborhoods, just like they did in white areas.

Neither the bus company nor the city commissioners would listen to other complaints and it seemed as if nothing else would change. The Montgomery NAACP was beginning to think about filing suit against the city of Montgomery over bus segregation. They needed to have a strong case and the right person to

At Rosa Parks Museum is this replica of a Montgomery bus like the one Rosa rode

Rosa Parks: Mother of the Civil Rights Movement

make it work.

In the spring of 1955, a teenage girl named Claudette Colvin had refused to give up her seat in the middle section of a bus to white people. Claudette was arrested. The Montgomery Chapter of the NAACP thought this might be the right case to take to court. Everything was going along fine until it was discovered that Claudette had serious personal problems. That was the end of that case. The members of the NAACP knew that they had to have someone who didn't have problems that the white people could criticize before they protested in court.

When Rosa got off from work on Thursday, December 1, 1955, she didn't intend to get arrested. She had her mind on her busy schedule and all that she needed to do. Rosa was working to put together an NAACP workshop for the 3rd and 4th of December, and there was still much to be done.

Her mind was filled with plans for the workshop as she went to Court Square as usual to catch the Cleveland Avenue bus home. She didn't even look to see who was driving the bus as she usually did. By the time she recognized Mr. Blake, she'd already paid her fare. Twelve years after he had put her off the bus on her way to take the voter test, he was still tall and

This historical marker stands at the site of the bus stop where Rosa refused to give up her seat

heavy, with red, rough skin. He still looked mean to Rosa.

Carefully, Rosa made her way to a vacant seat in the middle section of the bus. There was a black man sitting next to the window and two women across the aisle.

Rosa Parks: Mother of the Civil Rights Movement

The next stop was the Empire Theater and some white people got on the bus. They filled all the vacant seats, and one white man was left standing. Mr. Blake looked back and noticed the man.

He looked at Rosa and the other black people. "Let me have those front seats," he commanded since these were the front seats of the black section.

Nobody moved.

The four black people just sat there.

Mr. Blake spoke a second time. "Y'all better make it light on yourselves and let me have those seats."

The man next to the window slowly stood up, and Rosa moved to let him pass by. She looked across the aisle to see the other two women standing, too. Rosa took a deep breath, but she did not stand up.

Instead, she moved over to the window seat. *I don't see how standing up is going to make it light for me!* Rosa thought.

The driver saw Rosa still sitting next to the window. "Are you going to stand up?" he asked.

"No," Rosa replied.

Years later, people would say that Rosa didn't give up her seat because she was tired. That isn't true.

"I was not tired physically, or no more tired than I usually was at the end of a working day," she said. "I was not old, although some people have an image of

This bronze replica of Rosa sitting on the bus seat is at the Rosa Parks Museum in Montgomery

me being old then. I was forty-two. No, the only tired I was, was tired of giving in."

J.P. Blake glared at Rosa, "Well, I'm going to have you arrested."

Rosa Parks: Mother of the Civil Rights Movement

"You may do that," said Rosa.

Mr. Blake got out of the bus and stayed outside for a few minutes, waiting for the police.

Rosa tried not to think of what might happen. She knew anything was possible. She might be beaten. She might be arrested.

Never once did she think that she might be the test case that the NAACP was looking for.

"In fact, if I had let myself think too deeply about what might happen to me, I might have gotten off the bus. But, I chose to remain," Rosa said.

In the meantime, people were getting off the bus and asking for transfers. Many of the black people were afraid of what might happen. Others were angry with Rosa for her clash with the bus driver. They just wanted to get home.

Everyone remaining on the bus got very quiet. The little conversation that was going on was in hushed, low tones. No one was talking loud. Everyone was waiting to see what would happen next.

Finally, two policemen came. They got on the bus and walked up to Rosa. One asked, "Why didn't you stand up?"

Taking a deep breath, Rosa replied, "Why do you all push us around?"

Many of the black people who were left in the

back of the bus took a deep breath all at once. Was the policeman going to hit this lady?

He didn't. Instead, he answered simply, "I don't know, but the law is the law and you're under arrest."

As he picked up her purse, the second policeman picked up Rosa's shopping bag and escorted her to the squad car. One of the policemen went back to Mr. Blake and asked, "Do you want to swear out a warrant?"

Mr. Blake answered, "Let me finish my route and I'll come straight to the police station to swear out the warrant."

As they were driving to City Hall, one of the policeman asked Rosa again, "Why didn't you stand up when the driver spoke to you?"

By this time, Rosa was afraid to answer. She just stayed silent all the way to City Hall.

When they got inside, Rosa asked if she might have a sip of water. She was standing right next to a fountain. One of the policemen told her that she could. Then, the second one said, "No, you can't drink no water. You have to wait until you get to the jail."

After the arrest forms were filled out, Rosa asked if she could make a telephone call. "No!" she was told. Then, she was taken back to the squad car. The policemen drove her to the city jail on North Ripley

Rosa Parks: Mother of the Civil Rights Movement

Street.

Once they were inside the jail, Rosa asked again if she could make a telephone call. No one answered her. They told her to put her purse on the counter and to empty her pockets. The only thing that Rosa had in her pocket was a tissue, so she took that out.

Next, Rosa was taken to an area where she was fingerprinted. Then, mug shots—the term used for police photographs—were taken of her. A white woman who worked in the jail came to take Rosa to her jail cell. Rosa asked her, "May I make a phone call?"

"I'll find out," the lady replied.

Rosa walked nervously up the stairs to the second floor where the jail cells were. As they got to the top of the stairs, she stared uneasily at a door covered with iron mesh. The matron pushed the door open and led Rosa along a dimly lighted hallway. First, she placed Rosa in an empty dark cell and slammed the door closed. The matron walked a few steps away and then came back. "There are two girls around on the other side, and if you want to go over there with them instead of being in a cell by yourself, I will take you over there."

"It doesn't matter," Rosa said quietly.

"Let's go around there, and then you won't have

to be in a cell alone," the matron said. She was trying to be nice, but Rosa didn't feel much better. She was alone in jail, and she didn't know when she'd get to call someone.

As they were walking to the other cell, Rosa asked again, "May I use the telephone?"

"I'll check," the matron promised.

There were two black women in the cell. One of them spoke to Rosa. The other just acted as if Rosa wasn't there. The one who had spoken when Rosa came in asked her why she was there.

Rosa told her that she'd been arrested on the bus.

"You married?" asked the other lady.

"Yes," Rosa answered.

"Your husband ain't going to let you stay in here," the woman reassured her.

The woman took a dark metal mug from a hook above the toilet. She caught a little water from the tap and then handed the mug to Rosa. As Rosa finally got a drink of water, the woman started telling Rosa about her problems. She said, "I've been in this jail for fifty-five or fifty-seven days, I just can't remember."

"Why are you here?" Rosa asked.

"Because a man I was keeping company with got angry with me and hit me. I took a hatchet and went after him and he had me arrested," explained the

Rosa Parks: Mother of the Civil Rights Movement

woman.

"I have two brothers, but I don't have any way of getting in touch with them. That man wanted to get me out of jail, but only if I would go back home with him, so I just stayed here," the woman continued. "I've got a pencil, but no paper, or I'd give you my brother's number."

About this time, the matron returned and told Rosa to come out of the cell. When they reached a telephone booth, the matron gave Rosa a card and said, "Write down who you are calling and the telephone number."

Then, the matron dropped a dime in the slot, dialed the number, and stood close by to hear what Rosa was saying.

Rosa called home. Mama Leona answered the phone.

"I'm in jail," she said. "See if Parks will come down here and get me out."

"Did they beat you?" Mama Leona wanted to know.

"No, I wasn't beaten," she said, "but I am in jail."

Parks took the phone from Rosa's mother. "Parks, will you come get me out of jail?" Rosa asked.

"I'll be there in a few minutes," Parks promised. Since Parks didn't have a car, Rosa knew it would be longer, but she was glad to know he was coming. Just as Parks hung up the phone, a friend came by in his car. He'd heard about Rosa being in jail and came to Cleveland Court to see if he could help. Parks called a white man he knew to raise the bail to get Rosa out of jail. His friend took him to the man's house to pick him up.

In the meantime, Rosa was taken back to the jail cell. She thought, *I'll just have to wait until Parks can get here.*

Word was already out about Rosa's arrest. It spread through the neighborhood and the NAACP members like wildfire. Mr. Nixon heard it from a neighbor, Bertha Butler, who had seen Rosa being escorted off the bus. Mr. Nixon called the jail to find out what the charges were. No one would tell him.

Mr. Nixon tried to reach Fred Gray, one of the two black lawyers in Montgomery, but he wasn't home. So, he called Clifford Durr, Virginia's husband. Mr. Durr called the jail and found out that Rosa had been arrested under the segregation laws. He also found out how much bail money it would take to get her out.

In the jail cell, the woman who had been talking with Rosa found a scrap of crumpled paper. She wrote down both of her brothers' names and telephone

Rosa Parks: Mother of the Civil Rights Movement

numbers."

"Now, call them early in the morning because they go to work around six," she said to Rosa.

At that very moment, the matron came to tell Rosa that she was being released. As they were rushing Rosa out, the other woman threw the scrap of paper down the stairs where it landed right in front of Rosa. Rosa picked it up and put it in her pocket.

Virginia Durr was the first person Rosa saw as she came through the iron mesh door. There were tears in Virginia's eyes.

"As soon as they released me," Rosa said, "she put her arms around me, and hugged and kissed me as if we were sisters."

Rosa was relieved to see Mr. Nixon and Mr. Durr, too. They went together to the desk to pick up Rosa's purse and tissue from her pocket, and to get a trial date. Trial was set for Monday, December 5, 1955.

It wasn't until they were going down the stairs to leave the jail that Rosa realized how much being in jail had upset her. Just then, Parks and his friends drove up, and Rosa hurried over to the car. Never had she been so glad to see anyone.

By the time Rosa got home it was close to ten at night. Mama Leona fixed some food for her. Everyone was angry and talking about how something like this should never happen again.

"I will never, never ride another segregated bus," Rosa told them, "even if I have to walk to work."

Mr. Nixon looked at Rosa and Parks. Then he asked quietly, "Would you be willing to make your case a test case against segregation?"

At first Parks was angry. "I think it will be just as hard to get people to support Rosa in a test case as it would have been to develop a test case out of Claudette Colvin's experience," he said. "I don't want Rosa to get hurt."

Everyone talked about the question for a while. Finally, Parks and Leona agreed that it was a good idea. "We've always been against segregation and now we must be willing to fight it," Parks said.

Rosa nodded in agreement.

She would be the test.

The Boycott Begins

THE FIRST THING ROSA DID the morning after she was arrested was to call one of the numbers that the woman in the cell with her had written down. Rosa explained to the man what had happened to his sister. Then, she said, "She would like for you to come and see her."

"Okay," the man answered. That was the end of the conversation.

Two days later, as Rosa was walking up Dorsey Street to go to a meeting a woman walked up to her. The lady was dressed up and looked very nice. She was clean and had her hair fixed.

"Hi. How are you?" the woman asked.

"Fine," Rosa replied, a little bit puzzled.

"You don't know me, do you?" asked the lady.

"No, I don't," Rosa said honestly.

"I was the one who was in jail with you," the lady

said with a grateful smile. "Thank you for all of your help."

"I'm glad to see you out," Rosa humbly replied.

Rosa was in such a hurry to get to her meeting that she didn't think to ask the lady for her name or address or telephone number. That was the only time Rosa ever saw the woman she'd helped in jail.

On the morning of December 2, Rosa called Felix Thomas who operated a cab company. She was determined not to ride the bus again. She would take a cab to work.

Mr. John Ball, who was in charge of alterations at Montgomery Fair, was surprised to see Rosa when she came in to work. "I didn't think you'd be here. I thought you would be a nervous wreck," he said.

"Why should going to jail make a nervous wreck out of me?" Rosa asked. She went right to work.

During her lunch break, Rosa went to Fred Gray's law office. Ever since he opened his practice in Montgomery, he and Rosa often had lunch together at his office. Normally, she would answer the telephone while he ran errands. Today, his office was like a beehive. People were calling and dropping by to ask about a bus boycott and a meeting that the ministers of local churches had called for that night.

Rosa Parks: Mother of the Civil Rights Movement

Things were really heating up with the NAACP's case against bus segregation. Mr. Nixon was thrilled.

"My God, look what segregation has put in my hands," he said.

"Rosa Parks has worked for me for twelve years prior to this," he told reporters. "She is the secretary for everything I have going—the Brotherhood of Sleeping Car Porters, NAACP, Alabama Voter's League, all of those things. I knew she'd stand on her feet. She is honest, she is clean, she has integrity. The press can't go out and dig up something she did last year, or last month, or five years ago. They can't hang nothing like that on Rosa Parks."

Early that Friday morning, Mr. Nixon called the Reverend Ralph David Abernathy, the minister of First Baptist Church. Mr. Nixon thought that ministers could do more than anyone to get people in the community to work together. Mr. Nixon also called eighteen other ministers and arranged for a meeting to be held at Dexter Avenue Baptist Church that night. They wanted black people to boycott, or stay off of the buses, the next Monday in protest of the arrest and trial of Rosa Parks.

Mr. Nixon called a white reporter for the *Montgomery Advertiser* named Joe Azbell. He arranged to meet Mr. Azbell at Union Station to show him a handbill of what the ministers wanted to do.

"Can you get this on the front page?" Mr. Nixon asked.

"I'll see what I can do," Mr. Azbell promised. The story of Rosa's arrest had been reported in a small article in Friday's paper.

On Friday night, Rosa went to the meeting at the Dexter Avenue Baptist Church. She was a little embarrassed when she was asked to speak.

People asked her many questions about how she had been arrested and what had happened. Then there was a long discussion about what to do. A group of ministers formed a committee to draft a leaflet. It said:

Don't ride the bus to work, to town, to school or any place on Monday, December 5.

Another Negro woman has been arrested and put in jail because she refused to give up her bus seat.

Don't ride the buses to work, to town, to school, or anywhere on Monday. If you work, take a cab, or share a ride, or walk.

Come to a mass meeting, Monday at 7:00 P.M. at the Holt Street Baptist Church for further instruction.

The sky was dark with heavy clouds on Monday morning. That didn't seem to make any difference. The

Rosa Parks: Mother of the Civil Rights Movement

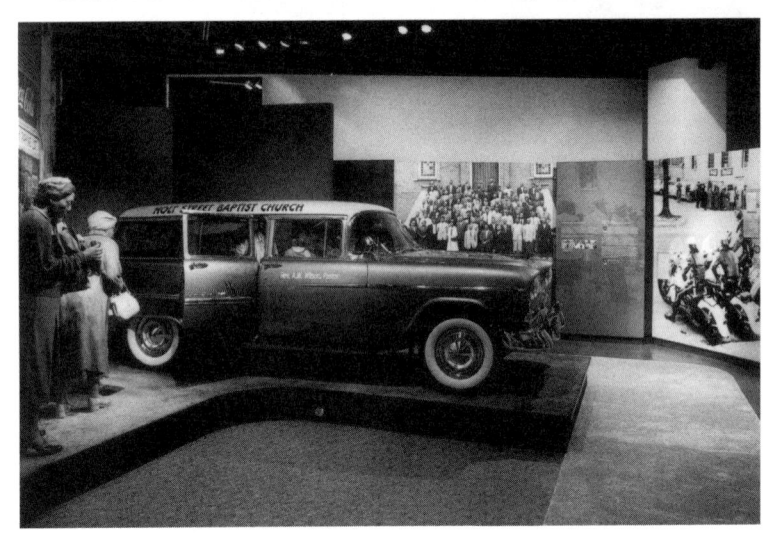

Rosa Parks Museum scene of Montgomery black women boarding station wagon used during bus boycott.

black people had had enough of segregation on the buses. The Montgomery city buses were practically empty. All of the organizers of the boycott were amazed that so many people went along with the plan. "We surprised ourselves," said Mr. Nixon.

Rosa didn't go to work that Monday morning. Instead, she went to the courthouse for her trial. Parks agreed to go with her.

Rosa dressed carefully in a straight, long-sleeved black dress with a white collar and cuffs. She put on a small black velvet hat with pearls across the top, and a charcoal gray coat. She picked up her black purse and white gloves. Amazingly, Rosa wasn't nervous. She knew what she had to do.

There were many people at the courthouse. Parks was not allowed to come in until he explained that he was Rosa's husband. The crowd spread out onto the street. A member of the NAACP Youth Council shouted out, "Oh, she's so sweet. They've messed with the wrong one now."

The trial was short. Mr. Blake was the main witness. A white woman also was called to the stand. She said that there had been a vacant seat in the back of the bus and that Rosa had refused to take it.

Even though Rosa knew this was not true, she wasn't allowed to say anything. In fact, Rosa wasn't allowed to comment. Her lawyers decided it would be best if she didn't speak at all. Her lawyers, Charles Langford and Fred Gray, entered a plea of "not guilty."

However, Rosa was found guilty of breaking the segregation laws and fined $10.00, plus $4.00 in court costs. The crowd grumbled angrily. However, this was what the NAACP wanted to happen. Now, they could appeal the case to a higher court.

After the trial, Rosa went to Fred Gray's office to answer the phone for him. It rang continuously. Rosa never told the people who were calling to complain about her case that she was the person they were calling about. She just answered the phone and took messages. When Mr. Gray returned, Mr. Nixon took

Rosa Parks: Mother of the Civil Rights Movement

Rosa home and told her she should plan to come to a meeting at the Holt Street Baptist Church that night.

Earlier in the day, Reverend Abernathy and some other ministers had met and formed the Montgomery Improvement Association (MIA). They elected the Reverend Martin Luther King, Jr., as their president. Dr. King was the pastor of Dexter Avenue Baptist Church. He was young and new to Montgomery. All of the ministers thought he'd be a good president because he hadn't been there long enough to make either strong friends or enemies.

The main thing to be decided that night was whether to continue to boycott. Some people thought they should quit while they were ahead. Others thought the boycott could only last until the end of the week.

Dr. King rose to speak. "There comes a time that people get tired. We are here this evening to say to those who have mistreated us so long that we are tired—tired of being segregated and humiliated; tired of being kicked about by the brutal feet of oppression."

He received loud cheers and applause for his speech. Then Rosa was introduced. She already had asked Mr. Nixon if she had to say anything. He said, "You have had enough and you have said enough and you don't have to speak."

So Rosa didn't speak. "I didn't feel any particular need to speak," she said later. "I enjoyed listening to others and seeing the enthusiasm of the audience."

The boycott lasted through that week, and then to the next. Churches bought station wagons, and volunteer drivers started taking calls from people who needed rides to and from work. After a while, there were twenty private cars and fourteen station wagons. There were thirty-two pick-up and transfer sites and service was provided from five-thirty in the morning until twelve-thirty at night.

The boycott continued.

Rosa and Parks lost their jobs. Parks resigned because the owner of the barbering concession where he worked issued an order that there was to be "No discussion of the bus protest or Rosa Parks in my establishment."

Parks replied, "I will not work anywhere where my wife's name cannot be mentioned."

Rosa was discharged from Montgomery Fair in January of 1956, but Rosa was not certain that it had anything to do with her arrest or the boycott. "I do not like to form in my mind an idea that I don't have any proof of," she said. "The young man who ran the tailor

Rosa Parks: Mother of the Civil Rights Movement

shop at Montgomery Fair had opened his own shop down the street...So, the explanation they gave me about not keeping me on was that they didn't have a tailor. They closed the shop. They gave me two weeks' pay and my bonus money, and I went home."

After that, Rosa worked at home taking in sewing. She also started traveling to tell about her arrest and the boycott.

The boycott continued.

Rosa served as a dispatcher, taking calls from the people who needed rides and then making the calls to the drivers of the private cars and church station wagons.

On December 20, 1956, a year after it began, a written order from the United States Supreme Court arrived in Montgomery. The Supreme Court ruled that segregation on the Montgomery buses was against the law.

On December 21, the black people returned to the buses. The boycott had lasted more than a year. Dr. King, Mr. Nixon, and Reverend Abernathy were going to ride the buses that day to show the first integrated busing in Montgomery.

Rosa planned to stay home and not ride the bus because Leona wasn't feeling well. Suddenly, there was a knock on her door.

"May I help you?" Rosa asked three white men who were standing there.

"We are reporters from *Look* magazine," one of the men explained. "We'd like to get your picture getting on and off the bus."

"Well, you'll have to wait a little bit," Rosa said. "My mother is sick and I am fixing her breakfast."

When Rosa got finished with her chores she rode downtown with the reporters. "They drove downtown and had me get on and off buses so they could take pictures," Rosa recalled. "James Blake, the driver who'd had me arrested, was the driver of one of the buses I got on. He didn't want to take any honors, and I wasn't too happy about being there myself. I got on two different buses, I guess, and each time they took pictures until they were satisfied. The reporter sat behind me each time while the photographer took pictures."

Integration of the buses didn't go so smoothly, though.

People shot at buses, and the homes of some of the ministers were bombed.

Anonymous callers threatened Rosa and Parks.

Parks slept with a gun by the bed just like Rosa's grandfather had done long ago.

Leona would call her friend, Bertha Butler, and

Rosa Parks: Mother of the Civil Rights Movement

talk for long periods of time just to jam the phone line so that the hate calls couldn't get through. After a while, Rosa's brother Sylvester made arrangements for Rosa, Leona, and Parks to move to Detroit.

"I'll see to it that you get settled up here," he promised.

In 1957, Rosa packed up one more time searching for peace and freedom. Rosa Parks currently lives in Detroit, Michigan.

Epilogue

AS ALWAYS, ROSA PARKS STAYED BUSY once she moved. Just as she, Leona and Parks got settled in Detroit, Rosa was offered a position at Hampton Institute, a black college in Hampton, Virginia. She decided to give it a try. However, there was no place for Parks and Leona to live on campus.

"My husband and my mother missed me a lot, and I just felt that it was too much for me to try to remain at Hampton alone and be concerned about them," Rosa said. So, she went back to Detroit.

She attended the Civil Rights March on Washington in 1963. In 1965, Mrs. Parks went to work for John Conyers, a congressman from the First Congressional District in Michigan. She started work for him on March 1. Later that same month, she walked in the march from Selma, Alabama to Montgomery to promote civil rights for black people. Mrs. Parks continued to work for the congressman until her retirement on

Rosa Parks: Mother of the Civil Rights Movement

September 30, 1988.

One of Mrs. Park's proudest accomplishments came in 1987. Along with Elaine Steele, Rosa co-founded the Rosa and Raymond Parks Institute for Self-Development. "Together we began a variety of programs that will help Detroit youth to pursue their education and create a promising future for themselves," Mrs. Parks explains. "I see it as a way of giving back to my people."

Mrs. Parks has a strong message for the youth of today.

"What message would I have for young people of today—of any race? Work hard, do not be discouraged, and in everything you do, try to make our country—and the world—a better place for us all...And remember: no matter what the circumstances are, it is best to pursue behavior that is above reproach, because then you will be respected for your actions."

Little did Rosa Parks know, that just one action, refusing to give up her seat on a bus, would cause her to be known as "The Mother of the Civil Rights Movement."

Roz Morris

For most of us alive today, in a very real sense, this journey began forty-three years ago when a woman named Rosa Parks sat down on a bus in Alabama and wouldn't get up. She's sitting down with the First Lady tonight and she may get up or not as she chooses.
We're thankful!

President Bill Clinton
Washington, D.C. 1999

Rosa McCauley Parks

February 4, 1913 Rosa McCauley born in Tuskegee, Alabama

1918 Enters school in Pine Level, Alabama

1924 Begins attending school in Montgomery

1929 Leaves school to care for grandmother

1932 Marries Raymond Parks in Pine Level, Alabama

1933 Receives high school degree

December 1943 Joins the NAACP. Elected secretary of the Montgomery chapter. A Montgomery bus driver forces Rosa off a bus because she refuses to exit and re-enter through the rear door.

1943 Tries to register to vote and is denied

1944 Tries a second time to register to vote and again denied

Roz Morris

1945 Receives certificate for voting

1949 Adviser to the NAACP Youth Council

Summer 1955 Attends workshop at Highlander Folk School in Monteagle, Tennessee

August 1955 Meets Dr. Martin Luther King, Jr.

December 1, 1955 Arrested for not giving up her seat to a white man on a bus in Montgomery

December 5, 1955 Stands trial; found guilty
Attends meeting of ministers who have formed the Montgomery Improvement Association
Start of Montgomery, Alabama bus boycott

1956 Arrested for second time for participation in Montgomery bus boycott
Loses job at Montgomery Fair department store

November 13, 1956 Segregation on buses in Montgomery declared unconstitutional by United States Supreme Court

December 21, 1956 Boycotters return to buses

Rosa Parks: Mother of the Civil Rights Movement

1957 Rosa and her family move to Detroit

1963 Attends Civil Rights March on Washington

1965 Begins working for Congressman John Conyers in Detroit

March 1965 Participates in Selma-to-Montgomery march

1977 Raymond Parks and Rosa's brother, Sylvester, die of cancer

1978 Rosa's mother, Leona McCauley, dies at age 91

1987 Found the Rosa and Raymond Parks Institute for Self-Development

1988 Retires from John Conyer's staff

February 28, 1991 Bust of Rosa Parks unveiled at Smithsonian

1992 Publishes *Rosa Parks: My Story*

Entrance to Rosa Parks Library and Museum in Montgomery

1996 President Bill Clinton presents Rosa with Presidential Medal of Freedom

1997 Receives International Freedom Conductor Award

2001 Rosa Louise Parks Library-Museum opens in Montgomery, Alabama

Roz Morris

About the Author

Roz Morris has taught students from preschool through eighth grade. She currently teaches third grade at Shades Mountain Elementary School in Hoover, Alabama. Mrs. Morris holds an M.Ed. in Elementary Education from the University of Georgia, and is certified to teach grades K through 8. She is a member of the Alabama Geographic Alliance, the state board of the Alabama Council for Teachers of English, and the 1999-2000 Alabama Textbook Committee for Language Arts.

Other Alabama Roots Biographies Available From Seacoast Publishing

Henry Aaron: Dream Chaser by Roz Morris
Hugo Black: Justice For All by Roz Morris
Paul Bryant:Football Legend by Sylvia B. Williams
Sam Dale: Alabama Pioneer by Tom Bailey
Jesse Owens: World's Fastest Human by Devon Hind and Kate Bergstresser
Daniel Pratt: Alabama's Great Builder by Tom Bailey
Emma Sansom: Confederate Hero by Margie Ross
Julia Tutwiler: Alabama Crusader by Roz Morris

Coming in the fall, 2002

A.G. Gaston: Visionary Businessman
W.C. Handy: Father of the Blues

To order more copies of this book or other Alabama Roots biographies, send 8.95 per book to:
Seacoast Publishing
P.O. Box 26492
Birmingham, AL 35260
Please print on your order the name and address where you wish the books to be shipped. Allow 15 days for delivery.
Orders also may be placed by telephone by calling 205.979.2909.